POEMS ABOUT YOUR ASS

184 Poems

BY

WILLIE B HARTIGAN

1

Your ass is the hottest,
and yet you're so modest.
You don't seem to grasp
it's the ass of a goddess.

Your ass is so quirky,
it makes my beef jerky.
I would stuff that ass
like a Thanksgiving turkey.

Your ass is so chunky,
it swings like a monkey.
Its size can entice
the most righteous of donkeys.

Your ass is so meaty,
that I want to breed it
and ship it wherever
big asses are needed.

Your ass is impeccable,
righteous, and ethical
with border security
tighter than Mexico's.

Your as is in France.
It flew in from Nassau.
Go put on some pants
so you don't freeze your ass off.

Your ass is magnificent.
Flashing it is a sin.
Please hide your ass,
or you'll incite an incident.

Your ass is a knockout.
All others are cop-outs,
'cause your ass is huge,
although you're not a fat cow.

Your ass is protruding,
distracting, imprudent.
Don't flaunt it in class,
or you'll flunk all my students.

Your ass has two hot buns.
They're round as a bonbon.
They're big as a beach ball
and white as a wonton.

Your ass is an idol.
No ass is its rival.
To all my attention
your ass is entitled.

Your ass is a liar.
It loves to conspire.
I smother your ass when
your pants are on fire.

Your ass is so brilliant,
I'd like its opinion
on whether to enter
your ass's dominion.

Your ass is your minion.
It has no opinion,
yet no one trespasses
your ass's dominion.

Your ass goes the distance
to aid your existence.
It never stops giving...
not even on Christmas.

Your ass does its business
in health AND in sickness.
I'll swear by your ass,
as your ass is my witness.

Your ass is humongous.
It blooms with abundance,
and I'm really glad
that your ass is among us.

Your ass likes to rumble,
and I'm ready to tumble.
I'll pummel your ass
till your ass becomes humble.

Your ass is 'da bomb',
so I thanked your Mom.
Then she showed me pictures
of her in a thong.

Your ass is all hairless
except in four areas.
If I waxed your ass,
I would not be so careless.

Your ass is my catapult.
It's so compatible
with my ambitions
and mission so radical.

Your ass is enthralling.
I'm constantly falling
in love with your ass,
'cause your ass is my calling.

Your ass is adhesive.
It's cheeks hug and squeeze me.
I can't leave your ass,
'cause your ass won't release me.

Your ass is so peachy
and raw like ceviche.
Go wash it with soap,
'cause I don't want to eat shit.

Your ass is a marvel,
because it's so artful.
It's quick to outwit
all the asses in Harvard.

Your ass is so smart.
It knows not to fart
whenever we're closer
than four feet apart.

Your ass is so pudgy,
that I'd like to judge it
by carefully placing
one hand on each butt cheek.

Your ass is so luscious,
it slips from my clutches
when you wear those blue jeans
that do your ass justice.

Your ass is rambunctious.
It bounces and lunges.
It strikes as a weapon
of massive seduction.

Your ass is real feisty,
but I neutralized it.
I banged it so hard,
that you had to go ice it.

If your ass could write,
it would make people think.
They would all wonder why
your ass writes with brown ink.

If your ass could read,
it would sit on a book
turning pages with cheeks
while the asshole just looks.

If your ass goes rad
and shits on my flag,
I'll hold my flag pole
as it goes up your ass.

If your ass talks smack,
I'll turn your ass black.
I'll hand you your ass.
You'll say, "whose ass is that?"

If I grabbed your ass
with a swift and bold swoop,
would you mangle my balls
or tell me that I'm cute?

If I took your ass
for a hike up that hill,
would that hike be high class
or just run-of-the-mill?

If I groomed your ass,
it would look fair and sleek.
You would not find ONE hair
in between your ass cheeks.

Your ass is conditioned
to bear big collisions
as you raise your ass
in your favorite positions.

Your ass is no slave, though.
It knows how to say "no."
It digs doing 'doggie'
but doesn't do anal.

Your ass is athletic,
and I am poetic.
I'll write your ass poems
with the hopes that I'll bed it.

Your ass gives me credit,
and I feel indebted
for all those fun times
when you ass let me wet it.

Your ass is a treat,
though it loves to do tricks.
And although it won't drive,
it will ride my broomstick.

Your ass is impeccable,
pure, and respectable.
Don't shake your ass,
'cause you'll make quite a spectacle.

Your ass IS a spectacle…
lavish and plentiful.
I will demolish your ass
with my testicles.

2

Your ass needs to shine,
and NOW is its time.
So letting it sit there
is surely a crime.

You ass has its pride.
It won't let things slide.
Without an ass warrant,
no one gets inside.

Your ass is conspicuous.
It makes my horse vigorous.
Its farts cloud my brain
like a train full of cigarettes.

Your ass is meticulous,
smart, and articulate.
Nothing gets past your ass…
not even little shit.

Your ass is remarkable,
bubbly, and bountiful.
I'll hold your ass,
but don't hold me accountable.

Your ass is insurable,
and though it's quite durable,
you'll need good ass coverage
for shit that's incurable.

Your ass relieves stress.
When life is a mess,
your ass is the pillow
on which my mind rests.

Your ass is immense...
so massive and dense.
Now, peel off those panties.
Let banging commence.

Your ass is attentive
and anal-retentive.
Before the shit happens,
it strives to prevent it.

Your ass looks so splendid
when it gets rear-ended,
'cause those big-ass butt cheeks
don't let it get dented.

Your ass is like candy.
It's not wholesome lamb meat,
but if there's a famine,
it CAN come in handy.

Your ass is tremendous,
and I'm its apprentice
till I fire your ass
and declare independence.

Your ass got the D,
though it barely could pass.
I grade on a curve
for good piece of ass.

Your ass is so disciplined,
that it doesn't miss a thing.
And I always whisper,
'cause it's always listening.

Your ass is committed
to keep shit within it.
It won't let shit go
unless new shit goes in it.

Your ass is so huge,
it has me confused.
I know it's just one,
but it looks like there's two.

Your ass has no pimples,
two cheeks, and two dimples.
And that's why your ass
is much more than a shithole.

Your ass is a darling
so cute and so charming.
When I lay both hands
on your ass, you disarm me.

Your ass is alarming...
environment-harming...
the reason that we must
abolish ass farming.

Asses are full of surprises
when their jeans are taken off.
They all change their shapes and sizes
shifting down, sideways, or up....

...But your ass is so tremendous,
that even after it shifts,
it stays stunning and stupendous
with your thin waist and thick hips.

If asses, like cars, had expos,
your ass would be a pink Lexus.
Pound-for-pound, your ass is sexier
than all the asses in Texas.

Your ass is so comprehensive,
so well-rounded, and so thorough,
it covers all of your bases
and even my big sombrero.

Your ass is a rebel
that cannot get settled.
It's as if you sat
on a boiling hot kettle.

Your ass is headstrong,
but it won't be long
till your ass submits
to my hips and my dong.

Your ass is so lively.
It's got me all smiley.
There's no other ass
of which I think so highly.

Your ass is uncanny.
It's such a fun fanny,
and I'd be all pervy
if you were my nanny.

Your ass has good curvature.
Lay on my furniture.
Lunge your ass towards me
as I take its temperature.

Your ass is refreshing,
and I count my blessings
advancing my hips
while your ass is regressing.

Your ass is so moving.
It's always exuding
that feminine flair
that I find so alluring.

Your ass keeps on fuming,
extruding, polluting.
Your ass should cut back
on the crap it's consuming.

Your ass is indelible...
far from forgettable.
Happily, I'll place
your ass on a pedestal.

Your ass is so stellar,
I sold my wine cellar.
Only in your ass
will I be a cave dweller.

Your ass is a specimen
of modern-day decadence.
Over ALL the asses
your ass must take precedence.

Your ass went to Hollywood
without the right attitude,
and that's why they're sending
your ass back to Malibu.

Your ass is impossible.
No ass is comparable.
Lower your pants
so my path has no obstacle.

Your ass is so optimal,
it's ALMOST impossible.
Now, watch my hips dribble
your ass like a basketball.

Your ass is downcast,
but this, too, shall pass.
The moment you twerk,
you shall perk up your ass.

Your ass is so pissed,
I've been handing out baskets
so we all can catch shit
when your ass blows a gasket.

Your ass is invigorating
watching it figure skating.
Gliding that ass over ice
looks so liberating.

Your ass is so visual,
I've made it habitual
to picture your ass
in my religious ritual.

Your ass is so precious,
it makes us all wretches.
We covet your ass,
yet we cannot possess it.

Your ass is a must-have.
I wanna have both halves
symmetrically sliding
underneath my nut sack.

Your ass is like moonlight
and hot air balloon rides...
the ass of a queen
who all asses are ruled by.

I liken your ass
to a barrel of moonshine.
It should not be legal
and leads to saloon fights.

I liken your ass
to the sweet Georgia peaches,
though thin fuzzy skin
isn't one of its features.

I liken your ass
to a big watermelon.
It rocks, and it rolls
and weighs more than a gallon.

Your ass is so hefty,
so right, yet so lefty,
that I lost my way
since the day your ass left me.

3

Your ass is not stupid, and
it knows that I'm Superman,
and though it may roam,
it comes home like a boomerang.

Your ass is my treasure…
a mountain of pleasure…
a valley of peace
and release beyond measure.

Your ass is so high-grade,
it makes my balls gyrate
when I raid your ass
like a greedy ass pirate.

If your ass gets jittery
and shows me hostility,
I'll bombard your ass
with "bombastic" artillery.

If your ass turns radical,
fiery, and flammable,
I will explode on your ass
like a cannonball.

Your ass is flamboyant,
yet never annoying.
Your skirt's the right length when
your ass cheeks are showing.

Your ass is so tropical,
it doesn't wear articles,
and even a thong
would be wrong and unpractical.

If your ass could fish,
it would catch a big bass.
It would jump in your thong
at the sight of your ass.

If your ass could fly,
it would scare all the birds.
It would hide in a cloud
and then shit out a turd.

Hold fast to your ass.
Don't you let your ass roam.
When you're with your ass,
you are never alone.

Your ass is gigantic.
It's got me enchanted,
'cause that added mass
gives your ass the advantage.

Your ass is galactic,
though you're not a fat chick.
Don't sit on my lips
if you don't want your ass licked.

Your ass stays on top of it
like darkness on chocolate.
If you let me lick your ass,
I'll eat at least half of it.

Your ass is phenomenal...
human, yet animal.
If I ate your ass,
would that make me a cannibal?

Your ass lives for passion.
It itches for action.
I will smite your ass
for the slightest infraction.

Your ass is so grand,
I can't understand
how all of it fits
in those tight little pants.

Your ass is so poppin'.
Your skirt is show-stoppin',
but when you wear drawers,
people's jaws just start droppin'.

Your ass is a mouthful...
the jewel of our household,
and in a food crisis,
it might be our last hope.

Your ass is colossal.
It must be a hassle
to shit with those cheeks
trying to cover your asshole.

Your ass is fantastic,
compressive, elastic,
and tougher than timber,
and rubber, and plastic.

Your ass moves the masses.
All races all classes
will follow your ass
till your bullshit collapses.

Your ass is a villain
that could make a killing,
but I've trained your ass
to remain a good citizen.

Your ass is so jiggly,
so wild, and so wiggly,
the streets can't compete with
your ass's activity.

Your ass is no wimp.
It can do its own pimpin'.
It punishes creeps,
and it leaves their ass limpin'.

Your ass is not subtle
with those two big bubbles.
Are those big-ass cheeks
made of silicone rubber?

Your ass has a rash,
and I think that it's tragic.
But if it should itch,
I will NOT help you scratch it.

Your ass has a purpose
underneath the surface,
so covering your ass
does your ass a disservice.

Your ass was a box of chocolates,
yet, once opened, it became
the spark that ignites my rocket
and the fuel that feeds my flame.

Whenever you ass goes shopping,
it struts with a subtle sway,
and with heels and soles clip-clopping,
your ass gets carried away.

I've seen 20 women pass...
all of them with nice big asses.
But comparing ass to ass,
your ass is far more fantastic.

If your ass were flat and narrow,
for your boobs I would still love you,
but your ass hides your whole shadow
at noon when the sun's above you.

Your ass is befuddling.
I find it quite troubling
to doubt my own eyes while
your ass size keeps doubling.

Your ass is astounding,
resilient, rebounding
when I grab that ass,
and I give it a pounding.

Your ass is notorious,
glamorous, and glorious.
Only your ass
makes my warrior victorious.

Your ass is medicinal.
It makes me invincible.
I will praise your ass
as a matter of principle.

If your ass could cry,
it would not cry with tears.
It would fart in a way
that would make its pain clear.

If your ass could drive,
it'd detach from your hips
and escape to the mall
without taking your shit.

Your ass is essential
and most consequential.
There's no other ass
that has so much potential.

Your ass is celestial
and extraterrestrial.
Looks more like a fruit
than it does like a vegetable.

Your ass is endearing...
the dearest of rear ends,
for nothing surpasses
your ass's appearance.

Your ass is so curvy,
so strong, and so sturdy,
that I'll ride your ass
at the Kentucky Derby.

4

Your ass smells like flowers.
It's fit to devour,
'cause each time you shit,
you immediately shower.

Your ass is legitimate.
It really does give a shit.
Though you turn your back on it,
you will not get rid of it.

Your ass sure has spice.
It loves to roll dice.
It stars in that Vegas show,
"Asses on Ice."

Your ass is so wise,
and I'm so surprised,
'cause I never asked
for your ass's advice.

Your ass is gargantuan,
and I'd like to count you in
a trial that requires
your ass and some margarine.

Your ass is a blast
when it passes gas.
I light up your farts,
and they flair with a flash.

My mule loves your ass.
He drooled when you passed.
So stay in the pool
while he's out on the grass.

Your ass likes to frolic
and go through my wallet.
It's turning me into
a dumb ass-coholic.

Your ass might talk fast,
but it will not screw me.
SHOW ME your ass.
I am from Missouri.

Your ass is a masterpiece
rounder than raspberries...
stronger than steel
like the ass of an athlete.

Your ass stabilizes
my energy crisis
when I frack your ass
for its natural gases.

Your ass is inspiring,
grinding, untiring.
Of all the earth's assess,
it's yours I'm admiring.

Your ass is so ample...
much more than a handful.
All asses should follow
your ass's example.

Your as is enormous.
I gravitate towards it.
I circle your ass,
'cause it has me in orbit.

Your ass is the bendiest...
so plump and so plenteous,
it goes on all fours
just to make my horse envious.

Of all your fine assets,
your ass is nicest...
USDA choice
and the Rolls Royce of asses.

Your ass is so dazzling.
Bring me some Vaseline,
so I can glide in it
and fill it with gasoline.

Your ass is most elegant,
and though I am celibate,
I will remember your ass
like an elephant.

Your ass is heroic,
though it may not show it.
It takes life's hard blows,
so your bones never know it.

Your as is a trooper…
much more than a pooper.
It makes my head shake
in a state of sheer stupor.

Though times might get rough,
I know we'll hang tough.
We won't go without,
'cause your ass is enough.

Your ass is 'bad ass'.
It earns all it has.
It has all it needs…
even makes its own gas.

Your ass is so useful,
so lush, and so fruitful,
it trumps all your assets
if I'm being truthful.

Your ass is so thick,
if we're poverty-stricken,
we'll deep-fry that ass
like Kentucky Fried Chicken.

Your ass is audacious...
without limitations...
dividing and conquering
The United Nations.

Your ass can move mountains
and activate fountains,
and that's why I'm happy
to keep your ass bouncin'.

Your ass is so comforting,
it drowns all my suffering.
I don't mind your ass
passing gas in my submarine.

43

Your ass is no quitter.
It keeps getting bigger,
and, though you keep eating,
it doesn't disfigure.

Your ass is so limber,
that you don't need fingers.
It softens my heart,
yet it hardens my timber.

Your ass has great firmness,
and I can confirm this
by shaking one cheek
as I squeeze and I turn it.

Your ass is determined
to be my good servant.
It bows to my dong,
and it longs to be squirted.

Your ass is a racket
however you pack it.
In jeans or in jammies
I'm ready to smack it.

Your ass is so polished,
that I must acknowledge
your ass looks as hip
as it as it did back in college.

If I smacked your ass
really fast like Bruce Lee,
would you chop off my head
or hop in bed with me?

If I slipped my hand
in between your ass cheeks,
would you push it away
or delightfully shriek?

Your ass has dimension.
It grabs my attention,
because it sticks out
in so many directions.

Your ass is symmetrical,
and that's not theoretical.
It's proven.
Both halves of your ass are identical.

Your ass feeds my habit
by letting me have it.
I never imagined
I'd be a crack addict.

Your ass is so pretty,
I think it's a pity
that less classy asses
should sit in committees.

Your ass is a village
that I'd love to pillage,
but getting inside
is a fight to the finish.

Your ass is so gorgeous,
that it could make fortunes,
but it's a free ass,
and it cannot be purchased.

Your ass is world class...
takes credit AND cash.
Would you be so bold
as to loan me your ass?

Your ass is sublime,
so fit, and so fine.
Your ass's advances
I cannot decline.

Your as is so wide,
I cannot decide
if there's enough sunscreen
for one or both sides.

Your ass is terrific
but not scientific.
Its tightness and wideness
defy laws of physics.

Your ass is an instrument
you'll learn to play instantly.
Just swallow some beans
to be in the ass symphony.

Your ass is so plump,
it has me all pumped.
I can't wait till Wednesday
to hit that big hump.

Your ass is well-rounded.
'Tu culo muy grande.'
It blocks the whole hallway.
There's no way around it.

Your ass is so brilliant
like one in a million.
It makes lesser asses
fade into oblivion.

Your mom is Sicilian,
your dad is Brazilian,
but with that big ass,
you can pass for a zebra.

I hope you find greatness.
I hope that you've laughed
with these dirty poems
that I wrote for your ass.